THE BOOK OF KALI MA

GRIMOIRE OF THE BLACK FLAME

FIRST EDITION

WRITTEN BY
M.G. CHAUHAN

MAPLE
PUBLISHERS

The Book of Kali Ma: Grimoire of the Black Flame

Author: M.G.Chauhan

Copyright © 2025 M.G.Chauhan

The right of M.G.Chauhan to be identified as author of this work has been asserted by the author in accordance with section 77 and 78 of the Copyright, Designs and Patents Act 1988.

ISBN 978-1-83538-637-8 (Paperback)
　　　978-1-83538-638-5 (Hardback)

Book Cover Design by M.G.Chauhan

Layout by:
　White Magic Studios
　www.whitemagicstudios.co.uk

Published by:
　Maple Publishers
　Fairbourne Drive, Atterbury,
　Milton Keynes,
　MK10 9RG, UK
　www.maplepublishers.com

WARNING:

It is strongly recommended that readers exercise caution before trying to follow the instructions outlined in this book. The rituals described in this book can be dangerous, and it is strongly discouraged for individuals who are emotionally unstable to attempt to perform them.

This book is not intended to be a substitute for the medical advice of a licensed physician. The reader should consult with their doctor in any matters relating to his/her health.

The author has made every effort to ensure the accuracy of the information within this book was correct at time of publication. The author does not assume and hereby disclaims any liability to any party for any loss, damage, or disruption caused by errors or omissions, whether such errors or omissions result from accident, negligence, or any other cause. No claims of paranormal or supernatural powers made. If you wish to apply ideas contained in this Book, you are taking full responsibility for your actions. Any use of this information is at your own risk.

All rights reserved. No part of this publication may be reproduced, distributed, or transmitted in any form or by any means, including photocopying, recording, or other electronic or mechanical methods, without the prior written permission of the publisher, except in the case of brief quotations embodied in critical reviews and certain other non-commercial uses permitted by copyright law.

कृं कृं कृं हिं कृं दक्षिणे कलिके
कृं कृं कृं हरिनग हरिनग हुं हुं स्वाः

"To the devotees of Kali, the preserver of Earth, who saves us from all the ignorance and the fear of death"

DEDICATION

This book is dedicated to

Oh, Kali Ma, Her Majesty and Mother of all Divine Wisdom, it is only through your grace and knowledge that this book has been made possible.

The night was sticky and oppressive in the Indian state of Gujarat in 1997. The air hung thick with moisture, and the sound of insects buzzing filled my ears. But something felt off, something sinister lurking in the darkness. At 3am, I awoke in a cold sweat, my body trembling with fear as I felt an eerie presence in my hotel room.

It was a dark and ominous night, and Kali ma's wrath was in the air. As she hunted for her intended victim, a piercing scream echoed through the neighbourhood. It was coming from the house next door.

The next morning, news of a disturbing incident spread like wildfire. The man living across the street, a well-educated engineer with four children and no history of mental or health problems, had inexplicably gone mad. He was taken away to a mental institution, leaving his family in agony.

But the truly terrifying part? It was all part of Kali ma's chilling revenge. The man had apparently committed some grave offense in the past, and now he was paying the ultimate price.

As the neighbourhood trembled in fear, whispers of Kali ma's vengeful powers grew louder. No one knew who would be next to fall victim to her wrath. But one thing was certain - the terror had only just begun.

As I lay there the next night, paralyzed with terror, the smell of death filled my nostrils, and my soul screamed with a primal fear that I had never felt before. The darkness seemed to have a life of its own, and I knew that I was not alone in that room. Something, or someone, was watching me, waiting for its next victim.

I tried to shake off the fear, to convince myself that it was all just my imagination, but the cold static electricity in the air and the flickering lights told me otherwise. I knew that I was facing something far beyond my understanding, something that was beyond human comprehension.

That night, the fear and the fire of my soul burned brighter than ever before. I was facing death itself, and I knew that I had to fight with all my might if I wanted to come out alive.

As I sat up in my bed, my heart pounding in my chest, I could feel the energy in the room shifting. It was as if the air itself was charged with an otherworldly power, a power that I could not comprehend. I tried to shake off the feeling of fear that was gripping me, but it was impossible. I knew that something was there with me, something that was not of this world.

As I looked around the room, I could see that everything was bathed in an eerie, blue light. The shadows seemed to be alive, twisting and turning as if they were alive. And then, in the midst of all this darkness and chaos, I saw her.

Kali.

She stood there, towering over me with her fierce and unrelenting energy. Her eyes burned with an intensity that was both terrifying and exhilarating, and her skin glowed with an otherworldly radiance.

In that moment, I knew that I had summoned her, that I had called upon the dark mother of the Hindu pantheon. But I had not been prepared for the intensity of her energy, the sheer force of her presence.

Kali was not a gentle goddess, not a goddess who would hold your hand and guide you gently down the path of enlightenment. No, Kali was a force to be reckoned with, a goddess who would challenge you, push you to your limits, and make you face your darkest fears.

And that was exactly what she did to me.

For what seemed like hours, I sat there in that hotel room, facing the goddess of destruction. She pushed me to my limits, made me confront my deepest fears and insecurities, and broke down every barrier that I had built up around myself.

But in the end, it was worth it.

Through Kali's fierce energy, I was reborn. I emerged from that hotel room a changed person, stronger, wiser, and more in touch with my true self than ever before. And I knew that I had Kali to thank for that.

Now, whenever I need guidance or strength, I call upon Kali. I know that her energy is not for the faint of heart, that it requires a deep commitment to growth and transformation. But I also know that the rewards are worth it, that Kali's energy can transform even the most stagnant and stuck parts of our lives.

So, if you are ready to face your fears, to break down the barriers that are holding you back, to tap into your deepest reserves of strength and power, then call upon Kali. Embrace her fierce and unrelenting energy, and let her guide you down the path of transformation and enlightenment.

But be warned: Kali is not for the faint of heart. Her energy is intense, her presence overwhelming. If you are not ready to face her, then wait until you are. But if you are ready to embrace her, then prepare yourself for the ride of your life.

Contents

Introduction 10

1. What should I offer to Kali Ma? 13
2. Ritual Preparation 14
3. Instruction's: 16
4. Mantras: 18
5. Spells, Rituals and Prayers: 22
6. Spell of Healing of diseases or illnesses 23
7. Spell of Increasing Wealth and money: 24
8. Master rite to communicate with the dead and bring someone to life by any means possible: 25
9. Spell to make someone desire and obsess about you: (use with caution) 29
10. Spell to take somebody wealth and luck and give it to you: (this can be extremely dangerous) 30
11. Prayer to Kali Ma for legal victory 32
12. Prayer to Kali Ma for confidence: 33
13. Prayer to Kali Ma to start a new life and gain wealth: 35
14. Prayer to Kali Ma to find new friends: 37
15. Prayer to Kali Ma to Inherit Money: 39
16. Prayer to Kali Ma for someone to return to you: 41
17. Prayer to Kali Ma for the protection of women and children: 42
18. Prayer to Kali Ma to win in all games of chance 44
19. Prayer to Kali Ma to make someone change their mind: ... 45
20. Prayer to Kali Ma to sell your house: 46
21. Prayer to Kali Ma to heal your pet: 47
22. Prayer to Kali Ma to bring your parents back together: ... 48

23.	Prayer to Kali Ma for any Wish or Desire:	49
24.	Prayer to Kali Ma for new Employment:	50
25.	Prayer to Kali Ma to bring money from all directions:	51
26.	Prayer to Kali Ma to make a neighbour move:	52
27.	Prayer to Kali Ma to make your new husband or wife appear in your life:	53
28.	Prayer to Kali Ma to gain fame and fortune:	54
29.	Prayer to Kali Ma to bring Peace and Tranquillity in your life:	55
30.	Prayer to Kali Ma to pass any Test or Exam:	56
31.	Spell for protection:	57
32.	Spell of Power and Success:	58
33.	Master Seal to gain superiority at work:	60
34.	Spell to protect women and girls: (Only to used by women)	61
35.	Master Rite to gain success at all costs	63
36.	Master Rite to Destroy and Paralyse all Enemies	65
37.	Master Kali Home Protection Seal	67
38.	Master Kali Rite to Increase Psychic and Magical Powers	69
39.	Master Rite to Call the Mighty Kail Ma to appear	71
Conclusion:		82

INTRODUCTION

I wrote this book with my lifetime's knowledge which I have gained from over 30 years of seeking the truth. Kail Ma is close to my heart and she has brought me to realisation of my weaknesses and strengths in my life. I felt it was time now in my advancing years to share this knowledge to the masses before I pass from this world. As a loner and someone who struggled with learning new things, I took solace with occult teachings and with my unseen Angelic friends. I was given these secret rites by Kali Ma herself in dreams and visions.

I was in two minds before writing about this dark forbidden knowledge to the public, I have always been seeker of the truth. no matter how it was preceded.

As I sat down to write about the dark and forbidden knowledge that I have accumulated over the years, I was conflicted. On one hand, I knew that this information could be life-changing for those who seek it, but on the other hand, I couldn't ignore the current state of the world. In today's society, political correctness and so-called "wokeness" have perverted the truth and destroyed the fabric of reality.

Despite my doubts, I knew that I had to share what I have learned with the public. This book is not like the others that you may have come across in your search for knowledge. It is not filled with useless self-betterment techniques that do nothing but waste your time. Instead, it is aimed at the ordinary person seeking to improve their life without the complex jargon that is often associated with the occult.

I have spent most of my life trapped in a cycle of mundane jobs and misery, always questioning my very existence. Is this all there is to life? Will I spend the next 50 years working for somebody else and remain poor for the rest of my life? These are the questions that plagued me for years until I found the answers in the occult.

However, I must warn you that some of the rituals in this book are dangerous and must not be performed for fun or curiosity. Please think carefully before starting any rite, and do not take any unnecessary risks. This information has never been disclosed to the public before, and I cannot stress enough the importance of caution.

Despite the risks, I have written this book with much love and dedication. Even though I do not know you personally, I wish you every success and happiness. I have tried to simplify all the methods in this book so that anyone can use them, regardless of their prior experience or knowledge. I can personally attest that all the techniques and secrets revealed in this book actually work, and I hope that they will be as life-changing for you as they have been for me.

Welcome to the world of the occult, where the veil between the seen and the unseen is thin and the mysteries of the universe are waiting to be explored. In this book, I share with you my lifetime's knowledge and experience in seeking the truth, the knowledge that has been gained from over 30 years of delving into the esoteric and the unknown.

As an occultist, I have encountered both light and dark aspects of this realm, and it is with great respect and caution that I reveal this forbidden knowledge to you, the reader. This knowledge has been close to my heart and has brought me to the realization of my weaknesses and strengths in life.

Knowledge truly is power, and I hope that the knowledge shared in this book empowers you to take control of your life and achieve all your dreams. So never give up on your dreams, and always keep trying. You will get there, and I will be cheering you on every step of the way!

Let's Begin!

WHAT SHOULD I OFFER TO KALI MA?

When it comes to making offerings to the Hindu goddess Kali Ma, there are certain traditional practices that you can follow. One such practice is offering food to the goddess, which is believed to bring good luck and prosperity to the devotee.

To make an offering of food to Kali Ma, it is recommended to use rice as the primary ingredient. This is because rice is considered to be a sacred and pure food item in many cultures, and is often used in religious ceremonies and rituals.

In addition to rice, Kali Ma also accepts red-coloured foods as offerings. This could include dishes such as kheer, which is a sweet rice pudding made with milk and sugar. Vegetarian dishes made with vegetables and rice are also a popular choice for offering to the goddess.

When preparing food offerings for Kali Ma, it is important to keep in mind her preferences and likes. For example, red-coloured sweets are said to be her favourite, and can be an ideal choice for an offering.

It is also important to remember that the intention and sincerity behind the offering are just as important as the food itself. By offering food to Kali Ma with a pure heart and intention, devotees can express their devotion and gratitude towards the goddess, and seek her blessings and protection in return.

Ritual Preparation

Before we begin, let's first understand who Kali Ma is and why performing rites in her honour is important. Kali Ma is a Hindu goddess who represents destruction, transformation, and liberation. She is often depicted with dark skin, wild hair, and multiple arms, each holding a symbolic item. She is a powerful and fearsome deity who is often worshipped for protection, strength, and the destruction of obstacles.

Performing rites in honour of Kali Ma is an ancient practice that has been performed by devotees for centuries. These rites are designed to harness the energy of Kali Ma, to help overcome obstacles, and to help bring about transformation in one's life. The rites are often performed during the dark of the moon, when the energy of Kali Ma is at its highest.

To perform the rites, you will need a few key items. First, you will need black and red candles. The black candle represents the darkness and the unknown, while the red candle represents the energy and passion of Kali Ma. Next, you will need plain writing paper and red and black pens. These will be used to write down your intentions and desires. You will also need incense sticks to help create a sacred space and to purify the area. Cooking oil or simple blessing oil is also required, which can be obtained from most occult stores. Lastly, you will need a picture of Kali Ma, which you can easily download from the internet.

Ritual Preparation

Before beginning the rites, it is important to find a quiet meditation room or space where you can perform the rites undisturbed. It is also recommended that you perform the rites after darkness, preferably after 3 am or 4 am, when the energy of Kali Ma is at its highest. This is because Kali Ma is known as the goddess of time and is said to be most powerful during these hours.

To begin the rites, light the black candle and the red candle. The black candle should be on the left, and the red candle should be on the right. Sit in front of the candles and take a few deep breaths to centre yourself. Once you feel calm and focused, begin to visualize Kali Ma in front of you. Focus on her fierce and powerful energy, and feel her presence in the room.

Once you have written down your intentions, light the incense sticks and let the smoke fill the room. This will help to purify the space and create a sacred atmosphere. Dip your finger into the cooking oil or blessing oil and anoint the paper with the oil. This will help to infuse your intentions with the energy of Kali Ma.

Finally, take the picture of Kali Ma in the centre and place it in front of the candles. Sit in front of the picture and meditate for a few minutes, focusing on the energy of Kali Ma and the intentions you have set.

Performing rites in honour of Kali Ma is a powerful and transformative experience. It allows us to connect with Kaki Ma.

Instruction's:

These rites are simple, yet dangerous once set in motion. Please heed my caution before proceeding. It is not about if it works or not, it is about do you want what you seek in the first place It is important to remember that Kali Ma is not to be trifled with, so stay focused on your intentions.

Before you start any of the rites, spells or mantras:

Light One Red and One black candle in your altar, put the picture of Kali Ma in the centre, light some incense sticks, make sure you are comfortable and relaxed.

Let your heart and soul open up to the Mighty Kali Ma! Rise up, lift your arms above your head, and with all the passion within you, proclaim aloud or silently (if there are others present in the room),

"Om Maha Kalyai , Namostute, namostute, namo! Om Kali Ma!"

Repeat the sacred words of Kali Ma three times, with each word spoken in reverence and adoration. You may feel a chill emanating from around you, the sound of hidden creatures scurrying in the shadows, and a scent of burning incense and flesh that fills the air.

Instruction's:

Have no fear as these sensations come to pass; for now, you have been bestowed a great blessing - an opportunity for communion with Kali Ma.

Speak forth Her blessed mantras and let your inner-most desires be known.

MANTRAS:

Mantra to Destroy Bad Luck:

Say with passion 10 times:

Om Maha Kayai,

Om Kring Kalikaye Namah
"Om Sri Maha Kalikayai Namah"

Mantra to bring protection from evil eye and black magic

Say with passion 10 times:

Om Kreem Kreem Kreem Hrum Hrum
Hreem Hreem Dakshina Kalike Svaha

Mantra to bring harmony and peace in your life

Say with passion 10 times:

Om Ucchista Ganapatayei Namaha

Mantra to bring money and blessings into your life

Say with passion 10 times:

"Om Shree Mahalakshmyai Cha Vidmahe Vishnu Pattaya Cha Dheemahi Tanno Lakshmi Prachodayat Om"

Mantra to bring love and new soul mate into your life

Say with passion 10 times:

Om Kreem Kreem Kreem Hum Hum Hreem Hreem Swaha

Mantra to get married

Say with passion 10 times:

Om Kleem Kalyayee Rog Mrityu Muktayee Kleem

Mantra to become successful in your Job

Say with passion 10 times:

Om Hraam Hreem Hraum sah Suryay Namah

Mantra to bring new job and employment opportunities

Say with passion 10 times:

Om Kaali Kankali Bhairav Samandar Jiye Piyali Char Veer Bhairo Chorusi tab tu Pujo Paan Mithai Ach Bolo Kali Ki Duhai

Mantra to bring good health and destroy all disease

Say with passion 10 times:

Aum Hreem Hreem Kleem Kleem Kaali Kankaali Mahaa Kaali Sla Khappar Wali Amuk Vyaadhi Naashaya Naashaya Shamanaya Swaaha

Mantra to cause someone to become insane and mentality disturbed:

Say with passion 10 times:

Om Maha Kayai,

Hoom Kreem Sarv Shatru Stambhinee

Ghor Kaalikaayai Phat.
(say the name of the person)

Om Maha! Om Maha!

Mantra to awaken your psychic powers:

Say with passion 10 times:

Om Maha Kayai, (say your name)

*Om Kreem Kreem Kreem Hrum
Hrum Hreem Hreem Dakshina Kalike Svaha*

Mantra to take wealth and fortune from a dead person: (Use with caution!)

Say with passion 10 times:

Om Maha Kayai, (say your name)

(say the name of the dead person, five times)

Om Namoh *Maha! Om Maha!*
Om Namoh Maha, Om Namoh Maha!

Mantra to bring misery and suffering to all enemies:

Say with passion 10 times:

Om Maha Kayai, (say your name)

Om baglamukhyae cha vidmahe stambhinyai cha
dheemahi tanno bagla prachodayat."
Om Maha!

Mantra to gain courage and strength

Say with passion 10 times:

Oṃ Āñjaneyāya Vidmahe Vāyuputrāya Dhīmahi| Tanno Hanumat Pracodayāt

Mantra to make someone obey and listen to your commands

Say with passion 10 times:

*Om Aim Hrim Krim Chamundayei Vicche Swaha
Om Maha Kayai, (say name of the person)*

Spells, Rituals and Prayers:

Make sure you preformed the opening ritual to Kali Ma before you start. Do not change any parts of the Spell, Ritual or Prayer at any circumstances!

In the realm of the occult, practitioners understand that every action has immense power and potential to cause a domino effect of consequences. Unlike moral contexts, where collateral damage is understood as unintended harm, in the professional occult this concept is viewed differently; there are no unexpected outcomes or unintended repercussions when dealing with powers beyond human control and understanding.

Every spell casted or ritual performed carries an enormous weight, like throwing a pebble into the ocean and watching it create rippling waves which then crash onto unsuspecting shores. Practitioners must accept the responsibility for all results of their actions, for even the most subtle spells can have dramatic effects. It could be gaining wealth or bringing an abundance of love, but it could also bring unanticipated financial losses or result in unfavourable health conditions. Nothing is off-limits and nothing is collateral damage; every outcome is simply part of the natural cycle of energy existing in the universe.

Therefore, when working with occult forces, practitioners know that every action has great potential to cause reverberations over vast lengths of time; there is no such thing as collateral damage in these practices, but rather a powerful connection to everything in existence.

Spell of Healing of Diseases or Illnesses

This is an ancient Kali Ma ritual of renewal, a powerful spell to evoke the healing energy within. Fill your bath with sacred herbs and essential oils, light some candles and let the warmth envelop you while you recite the words to draw out your inner strength and restore your spirit.

To start this healing process, you should make sure the bathroom is clean and have your own tub ready. Pour warm water into it and add powdered ginger and olive oil.

Light a candle then turn off the lights. Sit in the water, imagining any negative feelings washing out of you.

Speak words to ask Kali Ma, the goddess of healing, to assist you in getting better. Keep repeating them until you feel some relief. **"Om Kali Ma!" "Om Kali Ma!" "Om Kali Ma!"**

When done, get out of the bathtub and rinse yourself with cool water. Visualize all the bad energy leaving your body.

Place the candle next to your bed for a few minutes before blowing it out. You can repeat this ritual every night until the candle is gone and you are feeling better.

Spell of Increasing Wealth and money:

To attract a desired amount of money into your life, you can perform this simple ritual. Start by taking a clean sheet of white paper and writing down the specific amount of money you wish to attract. Make sure to write it clearly and legibly. Underneath your written amount, sign your full name.

Next, take a red candle and light it. Allow the wax to drip onto the paper, making sure it covers the written amount and your signature. Once the wax has hardened, fold the paper five times.

On the front of the folded paper, write the phrase:

"जय माँ काली"

(Jai Maa Kali), which means "Victory to Mother Kali" in Hindi. Don't worry if you're not familiar with the language; just do your best to write it as accurately as possible.

Finally, carry the folded paper with you at all times. You can keep it in a pouch or on your person while you go about your daily activities. It's important to keep the paper hidden and not allow anyone else to see or touch it, as it's a powerful amulet that should only be touched by its creator. By carrying this amulet, you are aligning yourself with the energy of Mother Kali, who is known for her power and ability to manifest desires.

Master rite to communicate with the dead and bring someone to life by any means possible:

(this can be extremely dangerous)

With fiery passion burning within, I wrestled with the decision of including this perilous ritual from the great Kali Ma, but in the end, my eagerness to enrich your knowledge won over my apprehension. It is solely your choice whether to summon the courage to attempt this mighty rite, which holds the power to communicate with the departed. As a testament to the depth of Kali Ma's divine wisdom, this knowledge was imparted to me in the year 1998, during my travels in the beautiful land of Gujrat, India.

Warning:

It is advisable not to take any risk as the consequences of performing this ritual incorrectly can be severe and irreversible. Therefore, it is recommended to perform this ritual at your own risk.

Stage one:

Light four black candles and four red candles and place them in your temple.

To communicate with the departed, write the name of the deceased person in black ink onto red paper. Include a strand of your hair or a drop of your blood on the paper. If possible, place a photograph or any object belonging to the deceased on top of the paper. Use some of your blood to anoint the belongings of the deceased. Put all the items in an empty shoebox. Finally, write the following rite on a white paper using red ink:

ॐ काली माता, जीवों की संवाद के माध्यम से जगत के अंधकार को दूर करने की शक्ति प्रदान करें। जो अपनी मृत्यु के बाद भी अधोलोक में उलझे हुए हैं, उन्हें तुम्हारे माध्यम से आशीर्वाद देने की कृपा करें। हमें शक्ति दें कि हम अपने पूर्वजों और उनके आत्माओं से संपर्क कर सकें और उनसे ज्ञान और विद्या प्राप्त कर सकें। हमें धैर्य, साहस और संतुलन दें ताकि हम उन्हें सही तरीके से संदेश दे सकें और उनसे अधिक सीख सकें। ॐ श्री काली माता नमः।

1. Place this powerful magical rite in the box too.
2. Add something which is sentimental to you and also include it this to the box
3. Add five black feathers, (you can obtain online)
4. Add eight drops of cooking oil to the box
5. Place a small mirror to the box
6. Carve your mother's first name onto some soap and place this in the box.

Next, seal the box with some packing tape.

On a full moon, after 3am, go to any graveyard and carve the deceased's name onto the ground and now bury this box without anyone seeing you. You only need to this once. Do not look back.

Stage two:

When you are back home, write the following rite in red marker onto a large full-size mirror

Master rite to communicate with the dead and bring someone to life by any means possible:

काली मा मृतकों को जीवित करती है।

Raise your arms above your shoulders.

Now, repeat this chant with passion:

Jīvitam Kuru! Jīvitam Kuru! Oh, Kali Ma!

Om Kaali Maata, jeevon kee sampaad ke maadhyam se jagat ke andhakaar ko door karne kee shakti pradaan karen.

Jo apanee mrtyu ke baad bhee adholok mein ulajhe hue hain, unhen tumhaare maadhyam se aashirvaad dene kee kripa karen.

Hamein shakti den ki ham apane poorvajon aur unake aatmaon se sampark kar saken aur unase gyaan aur vidya praapt kar saken.

Hamein dhairy, saahas aur santulan den taaki ham unhen sahee tarikke se sandesh de saken aur unase adhik seekh saken.

Om Shree Kaali Maata Namah. (name of the deceased person)

Oh, Kali Ma! Jai Kali Ma!

Repeat the name of the departed person with fervent passion and unwavering persistence until you receive a sign.

During the communication ritual, you will experience a presence in the room with you. The lights may flicker, and there may be a strong odour of decaying flesh. Furniture may also start moving without any reason.

Speak in your normal tone, whether it be in English or any other language that you shared with the departed. They will be able to hear you, and it's possible that they may communicate with you telepathically. Do not forget to close the portal once you have finished.

To close the portal, repeat this with passion:

Mata Kali, Apka Dhanyawad Hai. Aapki Jai Ho. Shanti se Jaiye

However, if you wish to further communicate with the deceased in the future, you will only need to proceed to Stage two of the ritual.

You can ask them any questions you may have. With patience, you will eventually see them in full view. In due time, you will have the departed person permanently in your life without requiring any further rituals.

Spell to make someone desire and obsess about you: (use with caution)

To draw someone into your life who will be infatuated with you and constantly think about you, acquire a photo or create a drawing of them. Ensure that it is connected to them in some way. Add some of your hair and blood to the image, being careful not to spill any blood on the floor.

Then, say the following in English:

Your Highness and Majesty, Kali Ma., place your black heart onto this man/woman (name of person)

Om Namoh Maha! Om Maha! Om Namoh Maha, Om Namoh Maha!

Raise your arms to the heavens, and shout:

Om Maha Kayai, grant me the power to enslave (name of person), if they refuse drag their soul down into the pits of hellfire! Let their screams fill the air as they burn in the eternal black flames of Kali ma!

Place the photo with their blood and hair inside an envelope and seal it tight. At precisely 4am or 5am, bury this offering in a graveyard and never look back.

Spell to take somebody wealth and luck and give it to you: (This can be extremely dangerous)

To attract luck and wealth towards yourself, acquire a photo or an article of clothing belonging to the desired individual.

Raise your arms to the sky and chant loudly:

Om Maha Kayai, (name of person), grant me their wealth and blessings. Let their soul bend to my will through the dark fire of Kali Ma!

Take their photograph or an article of clothing, and draw or copy out the magical seal from the book. Inscribe your name and the desired individual's name inside the box with a sharp implement, as you commit them to eternal servitude.

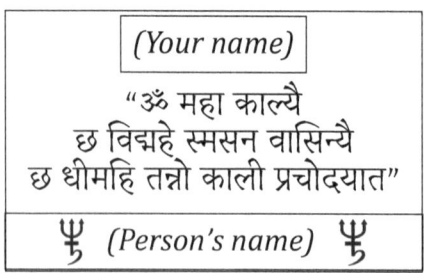

Spell to take somebody wealth and luck and give it to you: (this can be extremely dangerous)

Find an old pair of shoes that you no longer wear and place the magical seal and picture inside. Fill a box with newspaper, then add some strands of your hair and a few drops of your blood to the box. Next, use packing tape to securely seal it. Take the box out into the woods after dark and bury it somewhere deep. Once done, don't look back.

Prayer to Kali Ma for Legal Victory

In 2001, during my profound meditation to Kali Ma, I received this potent prayer.

Write this prayer on some white paper in red ink. You can keep it in a pouch or on your person while you go about your daily activities. It's important to keep the paper hidden and not allow anyone else to see or touch it, as it's a powerful amulet that should only be touched by its creator.

"ॐ क्रीं कालिकायै नमः॥ शत्रून् संहर मां देवि शीघ्रं विजयं देहि मे। विजयं देहि शत्रुत्वं देहि मे विमलं कुरु॥ अभीप्सितं सुखं देहि देहि मे परमेश्वरि। जयतां जयतां देवि संहारी त्राहि मां निश्चितम्॥"

Say this prayer with passion every day until you win your case:

"Om Kreem Kalikayai Namah|| Shatrun Samhar Maam Devi Sheeghram Vijayam Dehi Me| Vijayam Dehi Shatrutvam Dehi Me Vimalam Kuru|| Abhipsitam Sukham Dehi Dehi Me Parameshvari| Jayatam Jayatam Devi Samhari Traahi Maam Nishchitam||"

English Translation:

"Om, I bow to the Goddess Kali. O Devi, destroy my enemies and grant me victory quickly. Grant me victory and remove all enmity from me. Bestow upon me the desired happiness, O Supreme Goddess. Victory, victory to the Devi, the destroyer. Protect me, O Goddess, without fail."

Prayer to Kali Ma for Confidence:

Write this prayer on some white paper in red ink. Write this prayer on some white paper in red ink. You can keep it in a pouch or on your person while you go about your daily activities. It's important to keep the paper hidden and not allow anyone else to see or touch it, as it's a powerful amulet that should only be touched by its creator.

"ॐ क्रीं कालिकायै नमः॥ जय जय कालिका माँ, जगदम्बे कालिका माँ। शत्रु विनाशिनी, दुःखहारिणी, शरण्ये आयी माँ॥ माँ कालिका तू है सबसे शक्तिशालिनी, दुःख निवारिणी, पाप हरिणी, जय जय कालिका माँ॥ ओं ह्रीं ह्रीं श्रीं श्रीं क्लीं क्लीं सर्वानन्दायै नमः॥"

Say this prayer with passion every day until you feel confidence:

"Om Kreem Kalikayai Namah|| Jay Jay Kalika Ma, Jagadamba Kalika Ma| Shatru Vinashini, Dukhaharini, Sharanye Aayi Ma| Ma Kalika Tu Hai Sabse Shaktishalini, Dukh Nivharini, Pap Harini, Jay Jay Kalika Ma| Om Hreem Hreem Shreem Shreem Kleem Kleem Sarvaanandayai Namah||"

English Translation:

"Om, I bow to the Goddess Kali. Victory, victory to Kali Ma, the mother of the world. Destroyer of enemies, remover of sorrows, I seek refuge in you. Mother Kali, you are the most powerful, Dispeller of sufferings, destroyer of sins, victory, victory to Kali Ma. Om, I bow to the Goddess who brings joy to all."

May Kali Ma bless us with the courage and confidence to overcome all obstacles and challenges in life.

Prayer to Kali Ma to start a new life and gain wealth:

Write this prayer on some white paper in red ink. Write this prayer on some white paper in red ink. You can keep it in a pouch or on your person while you go about your daily activities. It's important to keep the paper hidden and not allow anyone else to see or touch it, as it's a powerful amulet that should only be touched by its creator.

"ॐ क्रीं कालिकायै नमः॥ जय जय कालिका माँ, जगद्म्बे कालिका माँ। त्वमेव माता च पिता त्वमेव। त्वमेव बन्धुश्च सखा त्वमेव। त्वमेव विद्या द्रविणम् त्वमेव। त्वमेव सर्वम् मम देव देव॥ जयतां जयतां देवि संहारी, त्राहि मां निश्चितं जयतां जयतां। अभयं दातुं कृपया जगतां, वीरान्यदीनां नाति-वीरानि॥"

Say this prayer with passion every day until your life improves:

"Om Kreem Kalikayai Namah|| Jay Jay Kalika Ma, Jagadamba Kalika Ma| Tvameva Mata Cha Pita Tvameva, Tvameva Bandhushcha Sakha Tvameva| Tvameva Vidya Dravinam Tvameva, Tvameva Sarvam Mama Deva Deva|| Jayatam Jayatam Devi Samhari, Trahi Mam Nishchitam Jayatam Jayatam| Abhayam Datam Kripaya Jagatam, Veeranyadeenam Nati-Veerani||"

English Translation:

"Om, I bow to the Goddess Kali. Victory, victory to Kali Ma, the mother of the world. You alone are my mother and my father, you alone are my friend and my relative, you alone are my knowledge and my wealth, you alone are my everything, O Goddess of all goddesses. Victory, victory to the Devi, the destroyer. Protect me without fail, victory, victory to you. Grant me fearlessness and compassion for all beings, Especially for the weak and the helpless."

May Kali Ma bless us with the strength and courage to start a new life and the abundance of wealth to live a prosperous life.

Prayer to Kali Ma to Find New Friends:

Write this prayer on some white paper in red ink. Write this prayer on some white paper in red ink. You can keep it in a pouch or on your person while you go about your daily activities. It's important to keep the paper hidden and not allow anyone else to see or touch it, as it's a powerful amulet that should only be touched by its creator.

"ॐ क्रीं कालिकायै नमः॥ जय जय कालिका माँ, जगदम्बे कालिका माँ। त्वमेव माता च पिता त्वमेव। त्वमेव बन्धुश्च सखा त्वमेव। त्वमेव विद्या द्रविणम् त्वमेव। त्वमेव सर्वम् मम देव देव॥ जयतां जयतां देवि विश्वहारिणि, पुण्यां श्रयतां मां सदा देवि शंभुवाहन। नवां नवां जीवनं सखीनां च सुखावहं, प्राप्तुं जगदंब त्वदनुग्रहाद्य मुञ्चति भूमेर्भारम्॥"

Say this prayer with passion every day until your life improves:

"Om Kreem Kalikayai Namah|| Jay Jay Kalika Ma, Jagadamba Kalika Ma| Tvameva Mata Cha Pita Tvameva, Tvameva Bandhushcha Sakha Tvameva| Tvameva Vidya Dravinam Tvameva, Tvameva Sarvam Mama Deva Deva|| Jayatam Jayatam Devi Vishvaharini, Punyam Shrayatam Mam Sada Devi Shambhuvahana| Navam Navam Jivanam Sakheenam Cha Sukhavaham, Praptum Jagadamba Tvad-anugrahadya Munjati Bhoomer-bharam||"

English Translation:

"Om, I bow to the Goddess Kali. Victory, victory to Kali Ma, the mother of the world. You alone are my mother and my father, You alone are my friend and my relative, You alone are my knowledge and my wealth, You alone are my everything, O Goddess of all goddesses. Victory, victory to the Devi, the one who destroys negativity, May I always find refuge in your holy feet, O Devi, who rides on Shiva's vehicle. Grant me a new life and good friends who bring happiness, By your grace, O Jagadamba, may I be free from the burden of the earth."

May Kali Ma bless us with the power to attract new and positive friends into our lives who support us in our spiritual journey.

Prayer to Kali Ma to Inherit Money:

Write this prayer on some white paper in red ink. Write this prayer on some white paper in red ink. You can keep it in a pouch or on your person while you go about your daily activities. It's important to keep the paper hidden and not allow anyone else to see or touch it, as it's a powerful amulet that should only be touched by its creator.

ॐ काली माँयै नमः।

हे काली माँ,

हम आपके समक्ष एक विनम्र हृदय से आत्मसात करते हैं, जो हमें अपने दैवीय अधिकार का दावा करने में मदद करने के लिए आपकी दिव्य हस्तियों को मांगता है।

आप शक्तिशाली और उग्र देवी हो, जो भ्रमों का विनाश करती हैं और धर्म की रक्षा करती हैं। मैं आपसे प्रार्थना करता हूं कि आप मेरी मदद करें, सभी बाधाओं को हटा दें जो मेरे मार्ग में आती हैं और मुझे जीत के मार्ग पर आगे बढ़ाएं।

मुझे अपनी विश्वास की शक्ति प्रदान करें, मेरी सही निर्णय लेने में मेरी मदद करें और मेरे दिव्य अधिकार का अधिकार करने के लिए मेरी हिम्मत प्रदान करें।

दैवीय ऊर्जा के अभिव्यक्ति के रूप में, मैं जानता हूं कि आपकी कृपा से मेरे लिए कुछ भी संभव है। मेरे सभी संघर्षों को जीतने और विजयी होने में मेरी मदद करें।

आपका आशीर्वाद मुझ पर हो, और मैं आपकी बुद्धि और कृपा से संचालित होता हूं। मैं आपको हृदय से धन्यवाद

Say this prayer with passion every day until you inherit the money you are owned:

Kali Ma my dear goddess, I come before you with a humble heart, seeking your divine intervention to help me claim my rightful place in this world. You are the fierce and powerful goddess, the destroyer of illusions and the protector of the righteous.

I pray to you to remove all the obstacles that come in the way of my path, and to grant me the wisdom and courage to stand up for my divine right. Help me to recognize and embrace my true purpose in life, and to follow it with conviction and dedication.

As the embodiment of divine energy, I know that your grace can help me to overcome any challenge and emerge victorious. Help me to tap into my inner strength and to trust in my own abilities, so that I may achieve my goals and fulfil my destiny.

May your blessings be upon me, and may I be guided by your wisdom and grace in all that I do. I offer my heartfelt gratitude to you, Kali Ma, and promise to honour and serve you always.

Jai Kali Ma!

Prayer to Kali Ma for someone to return to you:

Write this prayer on some white paper in red ink. Write this prayer on some white paper in red ink. You can keep it in a pouch or on your person while you go about your daily activities. It's important to keep the paper hidden and not allow anyone else to see or touch it, as it's a powerful amulet that should only be touched by its creator.

ॐ काली माता, जो हमेशा सबकुछ जानती हैं। आपकी कृपा हमें इस व्यक्ति को हमारे पास वापस लाने में मदद करेगी। हमें आशा है कि आप हमें अपनी शक्ति से संतुष्ट करेंगी और हमारी मदद करेंगी। कृपया हमें अपनी असीम करुणा दिखाएं। आदि शक्ति, जय काली माँ।

Say this prayer with passion every day until the person returns to you:

Om Kali Mata, who always knows everything. Your grace will help us to bring this person(name) back to us. We hope that you will be pleased with us and help us. Please show us your boundless mercy. Adi Shakti, Jai Kali Ma.

Prayer to Kali Ma for the Protection of Women and Children:

Write this prayer on some white paper in red ink. Write this prayer on some white paper in red ink. You can keep it in a pouch or on your person while you go about your daily activities. It's important to keep the paper hidden and not allow anyone else to see or touch it, as it's a powerful amulet that should only be touched by its creator.

ॐ काली महाशक्ति, संसार के उद्धारक, स्त्री-बाल के संरक्षक। आपकी दया से हम सुरक्षित हैं। आपकी कृपा से हमें शक्ति प्रदान कीजिए ताकि हम इस संसार के दुष्यता से लड़ सकें। हमेशा हमारे साथ रहें और हमें स्थायी सुरक्षा प्रदान करें। कृपया हमें स्त्री-बाल की रक्षा में आशीर्वाद दीजिए। जय मां काली।

Say this prayer with passion every day before going out

Om Kali Mahashakti, sansar ke uddharak, stri-bal ke sanrakshak. Aapki daya se hum surakshit hain. Aapki kripa se hamein shakti pradaan kijiye taki hum is sansar ke dushyta se lad sakein. Hamesha hamare saath rahen aur hamein sthaayi suraksha pradaan karen. Kripaya hamein stri-bal ki raksha mein aashirvaad dijiye. Jai Ma Kali.

English Translation:

Oh Kali, the great power, Savior of the world, protector of women and children. With your compassion, we are safe. Bless us with strength so we can fight the evil of this world. Always stay with us and provide us with permanent protection. Please bless us in the protection of women and children. Hail Mother Kali.

Prayer to Kali Ma to win in all games of chance

Write this prayer on some white paper in red ink. Write this prayer on some white paper in red ink. You can keep it in a pouch or on your person while you go about your daily activities. It's important to keep the paper hidden and not allow anyone else to see or touch it, as it's a powerful amulet that should only be touched by its creator.

ॐ काली माता, जो भाग्य और खेल के दौरान सभी से ऊँचा ऊपर हैं। आपकी कृपा हमें इन खेलों में विजय प्राप्त करने में मदद करेगी। हमें आशा है कि आप हमें अपनी शक्ति से संतुष्ट करेंगी और हमारी मदद करेंगी। कृपया हमें अपनी शक्तियों की विशेष रक्षा दिखाएं। आदि शक्ति, जय काली माँ।

Say this prayer with passion every day until you win big:

Om Kali Mata, who is above all in luck and games of chance. Your grace will help us to win in these games. We hope that you will be pleased with us and help us. Please show us your special protection of your powers. Adi Shakti, Jai Kali Ma.

Prayer to Kali Ma to make someone change their mind:

Write this prayer on some white paper in red ink. Write this prayer on some white paper in red ink. You can keep it in a pouch or on your person while you go about your daily activities. It's important to keep the paper hidden and not allow anyone else to see or touch it, as it's a powerful amulet that should only be touched by its creator.

ॐ काली माता, जो सभी के मन को अपने चरणों में आकर्षित करती हैं। आपकी कृपा हमें इस व्यक्ति के मन को बदलने में मदद करेगी। हमें आशा है कि आप हमें अपनी शक्ति से संतुष्ट करेंगी और हमारी मदद करेंगी। कृपया हमें अपनी असीम करुणा और शक्ति दिखाएं ताकि हमारी इच्छा पूरी हो सके। आदि शक्ति, जय काली माँ।

Say this prayer with passion every day until the person does what you want from them:

Om Kali Mata, who attracts everyone's mind towards your feet. Your grace will help us to change the mind of this person(name). We hope that you will be pleased with us and help us. Please show us your boundless mercy and power so that our wish may be fulfilled. Adi Shakti, Jai Kali Ma.

Prayer to Kali Ma to Sell Your House:

Write this prayer on some white paper in red ink. Write this prayer on some white paper in red ink. You can keep it in a pouch or on your person while you go about your daily activities. It's important to keep the paper hidden and not allow anyone else to see or touch it, as it's a powerful amulet that should only be touched by its creator.

ॐ काली माता, जो संपत्ति के सारे मालिकों का पालन करती हैं। आपकी कृपा हमें इस घर को बेचने में मदद करेगी। हमें आशा है कि आप हमें अपनी शक्ति से संतुष्ट करेंगी और हमारी मदद करेंगी। कृपया हमें अपनी शक्ति का आशीर्वाद दें ताकि हम सफलता से इस घर को बेच सकें। आदि शक्ति, जय काली माँ।

Say this prayer with passion every day until you sell your home:

Om Kali Mata, who takes care of all the wealth owners. Your grace will help us to sell this house. We hope that you will be pleased with us and help us. Please bless us with your power so that we can sell this house successfully. Adi Shakti, Jai Kali Ma.

Prayer to Kali Ma to heal your pet:

Write this prayer on some white paper in red ink. Write this prayer on some white paper in red ink. You can keep it in a pouch or on your person while you go about your daily activities. It's important to keep the paper hidden and not allow anyone else to see or touch it, as it's a powerful amulet that should only be touched by its creator.

ॐ काली माता, जो सभी प्राणियों की रक्षा करती हैं। आपकी कृपा हमें इस पालतू जानवर को ठीक करने में मदद करेगी। हमें आशा है कि आप हमें अपनी शक्ति से संतुष्ट करेंगी और हमारी मदद करेंगी। कृपया हमारे पालतू जानवर को अपनी शक्ति से ठीक करें और हमारे अंतर्दृष्टि को दर्शाएं कि कैसे हम अपने पालतू जानवर को स्वस्थ रख सकते हैं। आदि शक्ति, जय काली माँ।

Say this prayer with passion every day until your pet is better.

Om Kali Mata, who protects all living beings. Your grace will help us to heal this pet (name of pet). We hope that you will be pleased with us and help us. Please heal our pet with your power and show us the insight on how we can keep our pet healthy. Adi Shakti, Jai Kali Ma.

Prayer to Kali Ma to bring your parents back together:

Write this prayer on some white paper in red ink. Write this prayer on some white paper in red ink. You can keep it in a pouch or on your person while you go about your daily activities. It's important to keep the paper hidden and not allow anyone else to see or touch it, as it's a powerful amulet that should only be touched by its creator.

> ॐ काली माता, जो संसार के सभी रिश्तों का संरक्षण करती हैं। आपकी कृपा हमें हमारे माता-पिता को एक साथ लौटाने में मदद करेगी। हमें आशा है कि आप हमें अपनी शक्ति से संतुष्ट करेंगी और हमारी मदद करेंगी। कृपया हमारी माता-पिता को एक साथ लौटाने में अपनी शक्ति का आशीर्वाद दें। हमारी उत्तम सेवा के लिए आपका आभार है। आदि शक्ति, जय काली माँ।

Say this prayer with passion every day until your parents are back together.

Om Kali Mata, who protects all relationships in the world. Your grace will help us to bring our parents back together. We hope that you will be pleased with us and help us. Please bless us with your power to bring our parents back together. We are grateful for your excellent service. Adi Shakti, Jai Kali Ma.

Prayer to Kali Ma for any Wish or Desire:

Write this prayer on some white paper in red ink. Write this prayer on some white paper in red ink. You can keep it in a pouch or on your person while you go about your daily activities. It's important to keep the paper hidden and not allow anyone else to see or touch it, as it's a powerful amulet that should only be touched by its creator.

ॐ काली माता, जो संसार की सभी समस्याओं का संरक्षण करती हैं। आपकी कृपा हमें सभी कष्टों से मुक्ति प्रदान करेगी। हमें आशा है कि आप हमें अपनी शक्ति से संतुष्ट करेंगी और हमारी मदद करेंगी। कृपया हमें सभी दुःखों से मुक्ति प्रदान करें और हमें सफलता और शांति प्रदान करें। आपके आशीर्वाद के लिए हम आपकी सेवा में हमेशा तत्पर रहेंगे। आदि शक्ति, जय काली माँ।

Say this prayer with passion every day until your wish is granted:

Om Kali Mata, who protects all the problems of the world. Your grace will give us liberation from all sufferings. We hope that you will be pleased with us and help us. Please grant us this wish (name of your wish) and free us from all the sufferings and bless us with success and peace. We will always be devoted to your service for your blessings. Adi Shakti, Jai Kali Ma.

Prayer to Kali Ma for new Employment:

Write this prayer on some white paper in red ink. Write this prayer on some white paper in red ink. You can keep it in a pouch or on your person while you go about your daily activities. It's important to keep the paper hidden and not allow anyone else to see or touch it, as it's a powerful amulet that should only be touched by its creator.

> ॐ काली माता, जो संसार की समस्याओं का संरक्षण करती हैं। आपकी कृपा हगें नई रोजगार की प्राप्ति में मदद करेगी। हमें आशा है कि आप हमें अपनी शक्ति से संतुष्ट करेंगी और हमारी मदद करेंगी। कृपया हमें नई रोजगार की प्राप्ति में अपनी शक्ति का आशीर्वाद दें। हम आपकी सेवा में निरंतर रहेंगे और आपके आशीर्वाद के लिए हमेशा आभारी रहेंगे। आदि शक्ति, जय काली माँ।

Say this prayer with passion every day until you find a new Job:

Om Kali Mata, who protects all the problems of the world. Your grace will help us to obtain new employment. We hope that you will be pleased with us and help us. Please bless us with your power to obtain new employment. We will be constantly in your service and always grateful for your blessings. Adi Shakti, Jai Kali Ma.

Prayer to Kali Ma to bring money from all directions:

Write this prayer on some white paper in red ink. Write this prayer on some white paper in red ink. You can keep it in a pouch or on your person while you go about your daily activities. It's important to keep the paper hidden and not allow anyone else to see or touch it, as it's a powerful amulet that should only be touched by its creator.

ॐ काली माता, जो संसार की समस्याओं का संरक्षण करती हैं। आपकी कृपा हमें संपूर्ण दिशाओं से धन प्राप्त करने में मदद करेगी। हमें आशा है कि आप हमें अपनी शक्ति से संतुष्ट करेंगी और हमारी मदद करेंगी। कृपया हमें संपूर्ण दिशाओं से धन की वर्षा करने में अपनी शक्ति का आशीर्वाद दें। हम आपकी सेवा में निरंतर रहेंगे और आपके आशीर्वाद के लिए हमेशा आभारी रहेंगे। आदि शक्ति, जय काली माँ।

Say this prayer with passion every day until your wish is granted:

Om Kali Mata, who protects all the problems of the world. Your grace will help us to obtain wealth from all directions. We hope that you will be pleased with us and help us. Please bless us with your power to rain down wealth from all directions. We will be constantly in your service and always grateful for your blessings. Adi Shakti, Jai Kali Ma.

Prayer to Kali Ma to make a neighbour move:

Write this prayer on some white paper in red ink. Write this prayer on some white paper in red ink. You can keep it in a pouch or on your person while you go about your daily activities. It's important to keep the paper hidden and not allow anyone else to see or touch it, as it's a powerful amulet that should only be touched by its creator.

ॐ काली माता, आप मेरी मदद् करें कि मैं अपने अतीत से हटकर आगे बढ़ सकूं। मेरी आत्मा को शक्ति दें कि मैं जीवन के अगले अध्याय में संतुष्ट रहूं। मेरी भावनाओं को शांति दें और मुझे उन लोगों के लिए क्षमा करने की शक्ति दें जो मेरे अतीत में मेरे खिलाफ थे। कृपया मुझे अपनी आशीर्वाद दें जो मुझे मेरे जीवन के अगले चरण में आगे बढ़ने में मदद करेगा। धन्यवाद।

Say this prayer with passion every day until your wish is granted:

Om Kali Mata, please help my neighbour move away from my life and move forward in their life. Give them strength to be content in the next chapter of their life. Grant them peace of mind and the ability to forgive those who were against me in the past. Please bless them with your grace that will help them move forward in the next phase of their life. Thank you, my Kali Ma!

Prayer to Kali Ma to make your new husband or wife appear in your life:

Write this prayer on some white paper in red ink. Write this prayer on some white paper in red ink. You can keep it in a pouch or on your person while you go about your daily activities. It's important to keep the paper hidden and not allow anyone else to see or touch it, as it's a powerful amulet that should only be touched by its creator.

ॐ काली माता, आपसे अनुरोध है कि आप मेरी मदद करें और मेरे जीवन में एक नया पति / पत्नी आने की कृपा करें। मुझे उस व्यक्ति के लिए आशीर्वाद दें जो मेरे जीवन का साथी बन सके। कृपया मुझे उस व्यक्ति से मिलवाएं जो मुझे धैर्य, प्यार और सहयोग का साथ देने के लिए तैयार हो। मुझे उस व्यक्ति को अपने जीवन में स्वीकार करने की शक्ति दें और मुझे उसके साथ जीवन का अगला अध्याय शुरू करने के लिए उत्साह दें। धन्यवाद।

Say this prayer with passion every day until your new love appears in your life:

Om Kali Mata, I humbly request you to help me find a new husband/wife in my life. Please bless me with a partner who can accompany me in my journey of life. Please guide me to meet someone who is willing to give me patience, love, and support. Grant me the strength to accept this person in my life and give me the enthusiasm to start a new chapter of my life with them. Thank you.

Prayer to Kali Ma to gain fame and fortune:

Write this prayer on some white paper in red ink. Write this prayer on some white paper in red ink. You can keep it in a pouch or on your person while you go about your daily activities. It's important to keep the paper hidden and not allow anyone else to see or touch it, as it's a powerful amulet that should only be touched by its creator.

ॐ काली माता, आपसे अनुरोध है कि आप मुझे नाम और धन की प्राप्ति में मदद करें। मेरी कृपा करें और मेरी योग्यता के अनुसार मुझे सफलता का मार्ग दिखाएं। कृपया मुझे अधिक उच्च स्थान और सम्मान प्रदान करें और मेरी धन की आवश्यकताओं को पूरा करने में मेरी मदद करें। मुझे आपके आशीर्वाद की आवश्यकता है। धन्यवाद

Say this prayer with passion every day until fame appears in your life:

Om Kali Mata, I humbly request you to help me in gaining fame and fortune. Please bless me and guide me towards the path of success as per my capability. Please provide me with more prominent positions and respect and help me fulfil my financial needs. I need your blessings. Thank you.

Prayer to Kali Ma to bring Peace and Tranquillity in your life:

Write this prayer on some white paper in red ink. Write this prayer on some white paper in red ink. You can keep it in a pouch or on your person while you go about your daily activities. It's important to keep the paper hidden and not allow anyone else to see or touch it, as it's a powerful amulet that should only be touched by its creator.

> ॐ काली माता, आपसे अनुरोध है कि आप मेरी ज़िंदगी में शांति और शांतिपूर्णता लाएं। कृपया मुझे उन उपायों का बताएं जो मुझे शांति और आराम का अनुभव करने में मदद करें। मुझे ध्यान और मेधा की शक्ति दें जो मुझे अपने जीवन के सभी क्षेत्रों में सफलता और शांति प्रदान करें। कृपया मेरे सभी संबंधित विषयों को शांत रखें और मुझे आपकी शांति की आवश्यकता है। धन्यवाद।

Say this prayer with passion every day until your wish is granted:

Om Kali Mata, I humbly request you to bring peace and tranquillity in my life. Please guide me towards the methods that help me experience peace and relaxation. Please grant me the power of focus and intelligence that brings success and peace in all areas of my life. Please keep all my relevant matters calm, and I need your peace. Thank you.

Prayer to Kali Ma to pass any Test or Exam:

Write this prayer on some white paper in red ink. Write this prayer on some white paper in red ink. You can keep it in a pouch or on your person while you go about your daily activities. It's important to keep the paper hidden and not allow anyone else to see or touch it, as it's a powerful amulet that should only be touched by its creator.

ॐ काली माता, आपसे अनुरोध है कि आप मेरी परीक्षाओं में सफलता दिलाने में मेरी मदद करें। कृपया मेरी ध्यान और समझ को बढ़ाएं और मेरी सभी बाधाओं को दूर करने में मेरी मदद करें। कृपया मेरे अध्ययन को सफल बनाएं और मेरी समझ को परीक्षा के समय तेज़ करें। मुझे उचित दिशा और भावनाओं को चुनने में मेरी मदद करें जो मुझे सफलता प्रदान करें। मैं आपकी आशीर्वाद की प्रतीक्षा करता हूं। धन्यवाद।

Say this prayer with passion every day until you have passed your test or exam:

Om Kali Mata, I humbly request you to help me succeed in my tests and examinations. Please increase my focus and understanding and help me overcome all obstacles. Please make my studies successful and sharpen my mind during the exams. Please guide me towards the right direction and emotions that bring me success. I await your blessings. Thank you.

Spell for protection:

Say:

Om Namoh *Maha! Om Maha!*
Om Namoh Maha, Om Namoh Maha!

"Om Krim Kali"

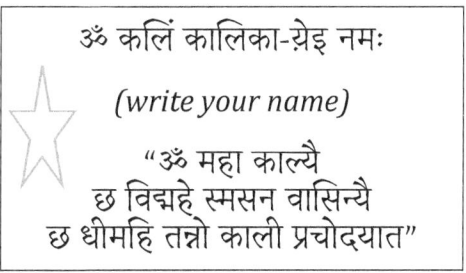

You only need to perform this one time. Now, draw or photocopy the above magical seal the best you can, place in an envelope or pouch, carry at all times on your person. Do not allow anyone to touch or see this powerful amulet. It will protect you from all evil and black magick. It will also give you protection form evil people, demons and those whom wishes to harm you.

Spell of Power and Success:

To cast this spell, it's recommended to do so during a full moon, waxing moon, or on a Friday. Begin by using a red pen to draw a large pentagram on your paper.

Ensure that the star is pointing upwards and not downwards. In the centre of the pentagram, write the words:

ॐ कलिं कालिका-स्त्रेइ नम

Next, tear up some curry or mint leaves and add them, along with dried sage, to the pentagram.

Place a candle in a holder on top of the herbs and light it.

Speak the following words: "Kali Ma, hear my plea. Make me strong and powerful. Hear me, my mighty Kali Ma, hear me!"

Allow the red tea candle to burn all the way down. Then, take the paper with the herbs to the nearest window. Carefully light the paper, collect the ash, and blow it out the window.

Master Seal to Gain Superiority at Work:

In the summer of 1999, I received an exceptional and mysterious charm from Kali Ma while in a trance-like state during a meditation session. This magical Seal promised to grant me power and success in my professional endeavours.

To cast this spell, it's recommended to do so during a full moon, waxing moon, or on a Wednesday. Begin by using a red pen to draw the seal below:

You only need to perform this one time. Now, draw or photocopy the above magical seal the best you can, place in an envelope or pouch, carry at all times on your person. Do not allow anyone to touch or see this powerful amulet. It will protect you from all those whom wishes you harm and give you power over others at work.

Spell to protect women and girls: (Only to used by women)

I was gifted this magical seal by Kali Ma herself in 1997 during a deep meditation, and it is meant to be used exclusively by women and young girls. Despite the current of political correctness that runs through our age, women in India still face immense danger from men, and police corruption is widespread. In these moments of peril, Kali Ma stands as a true protector of women's rights!

To cast this spell work, it's recommended to do so during a full moon, waxing moon, or on a Saturday. Begin by using a red and black pen to draw the seal below:

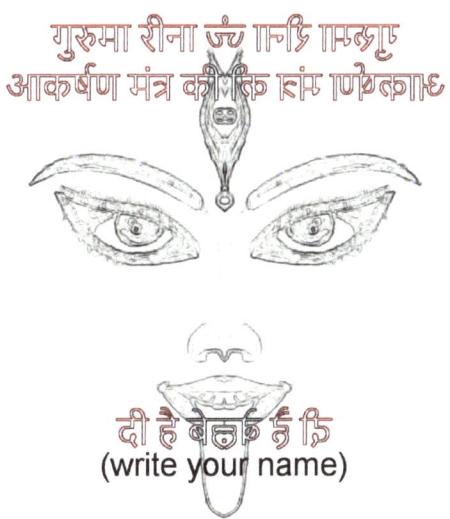
(write your name)

Raise your voice to the heavens, and cry out with passion:

Om Kali Ma! "Om Klim Kalika-Yei Namaha"

Repeat the chant until it echoes through the air, letting every living creature feel its power. Carve the magical seal into existence with a flourish and bow down in reverence as you offer up your prayers.

You only need to perform this one time. Now, draw or photocopy the above magical seal the best you can, place in an envelope or pouch, carry at all times on your person. Do not allow anyone to touch or see this powerful amulet. It will protect you from all those whom wishes you harm. You may feel an unseen supernatural force watching you.

Master Rite to gain success at all costs

To cast this spell, it's recommended to do so during a full moon, waxing moon, or on a Monday. Begin by using a black pen to draw the seal below:

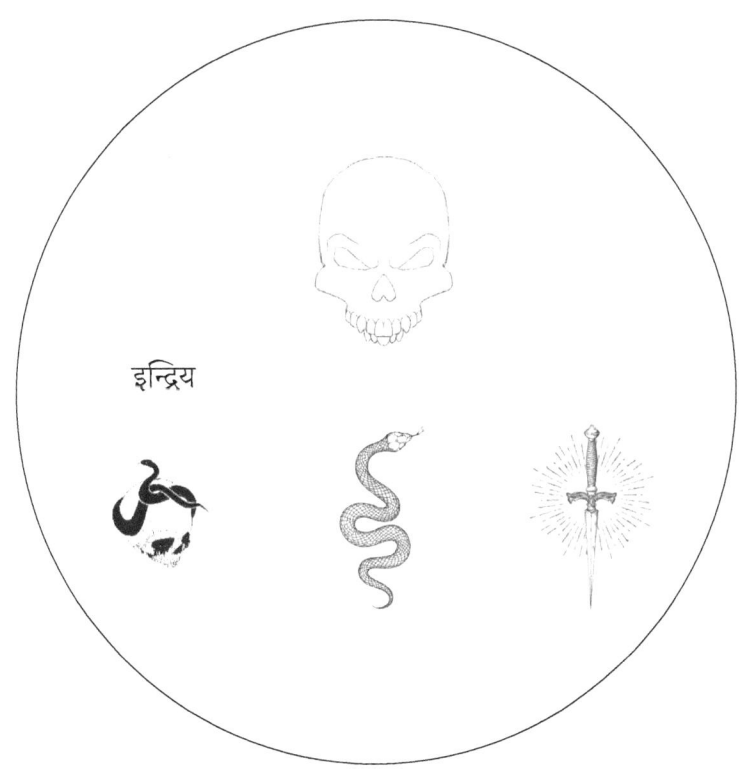

Unleash a deafening cry to the heavens, calling out with rapture:

Om Namoh Maha! Om Maha!

Allow the chant to rattle through the sky, spreading its might throughout all living beings. Take your pen and carve the sacred seal onto paper or any object with a determined thrust, then dip down in veneration and offer up your reverence vociferously.

You only need to perform this one time. Now, draw or photocopy the above magical seal the best you can, place in an envelope or pouch, carry at all times on your person. Do not allow anyone to touch or see this powerful amulet.

Master Rite to Destroy and Paralyse all Enemies

In 1998, during a profound meditation, Kali Ma herself presented me with a mystical seal. This seal is intended to be utilized only as a final option, after all peaceful avenues have been exhausted.

It is important to exercise prudence when using this seal, as once initiated, it would be exceedingly difficult to halt its effects.

Before invoking the deadly fury of Kali Ma upon your adversaries, it is crucial to carefully consider your actions.

For best results, perform this spell during a full moon, waxing moon, or on a Sunday. Use a red or black pen to draw the seal below:

You only need to perform this one time. Now, draw the magical seal the best you can

Gather some photos or articles to show Kali ma your intentions. Add a few strands of your hair and a drop of blood to the seal, being cautious not to let any blood fall onto the ground.

Repeat the following incantation:

Om Namoh Maha! Om Maha! Om Namoh Maha, Om Namoh Maha!

Then, extend your arms and say:

Maha Kayai, make my enemies burn and take their souls and drag them to the pits of hell and fire, till they spend eternity in black flames of Kali ma!

Secure the seal with some of your hair into an envelope and seal it shut. Now bury this in the ground between 3am or 4 am. Once buried, do not look back.

Master Kali Home Protection Seal

In the winter of 1998, while I was in a profound state of meditation, I was bestowed with a mystical seal by the powerful Kali Ma. Beware those who dare to harm you or your loved ones, for they shall face the wrathful fury of Kali Ma herself! This remarkable seal is intended to safeguard your home against intruders and is particularly useful in the small villages of India, where crime and danger lurk at every turn. India is a land of stark contrasts, with two distinct realities: one for the wealthy and influential, and another for the impoverished. In a society where money and power hold sway, those lacking these resources are often overlooked by the authorities. Oh, what greater power could there be than to possess an unseen and all-powerful shield form Her Majesty Kali Ma, that renders her completely invincible and untouchable by any force in this world!

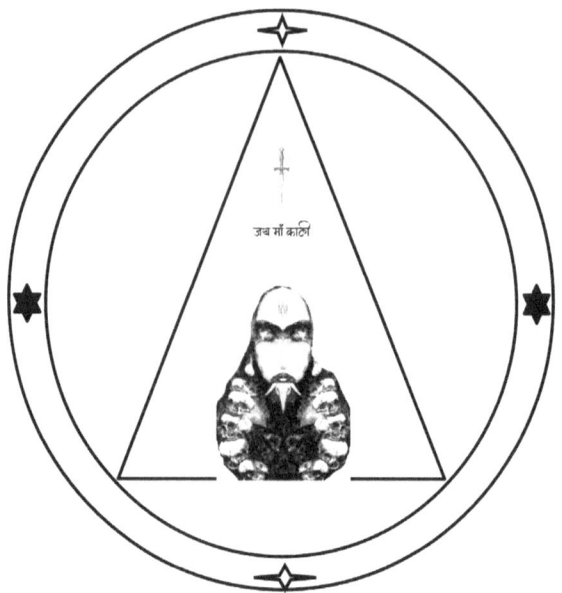

With all the passion in your heart, raise your voice to the heavens and let out a powerful cry:

Utter the sacred words with deep reverence:

"OM KALI MA! OM KLIM KALIKA-YEI NAMAHA!"

Keep repeating the chant with all your might until it reverberates through the air, permeating every living being with its profound energy. With a graceful flourish, carve the magical seal into existence and bow down in complete submission, offering your heartfelt prayers to the Divine.

This is a sacred ritual that needs to be performed only once. Get ready to draw or photocopy the mystical seal that you see above to the best of your abilities. Once you have it, place it in a concealed location near your front door, and guard it with your life. Do not let anyone lay eyes on this mighty talisman, for its power is not to be trifled with.

Master Kali Rite to Increase Psychic and Magical Powers

In the autumn of 1997, while in a state of deep meditation, I was granted a mystical seal by the powerful Kali Ma. This seal is said to bestow psychic abilities and the power to transmit telepathic messages to whomever one chooses. The symbol has the potential to unlock and amplify one's psychic abilities, empowering the possessor to communicate telepathically with anyone they wish. With the guidance and support of Kali Ma, individuals can delve into the unknown and gain a greater comprehension of mystical sciences. Additionally, Kali Ma's divine intervention may awaken the mind to the concealed and esoteric knowledge that has been lost to time. This profound gift can enable people to unravel the secrets of the universe and explore the depths of human consciousness, leading to a transformative journey of self-discovery and enlightenment.

With all the passion in your heart, raise your voice to the heavens and let out a powerful cry:

Utter the sacred words with deep reverence:

Om Namoh Maha! Om Maha!

Keep repeating the chant with all your might until it reverberates through the air, permeating every living being with its profound energy. With a graceful flourish, carve the magical seal into existence and bow down in complete submission, offering your heartfelt prayers to the Divine.

This is a sacred rite that needs to be performed only once. Get ready to draw or photocopy the mystical seal that you see above to the best of your abilities. place in an envelope or pouch, carry at all times on your person. Do not allow anyone to touch or see this powerful amulet.

Master Rite to Call the Mighty Kail Ma to appear

This rite is probably the most difficult to perform. It took me many years to perfect, with many trials and errors, but I have finally done it.

The original rite from Mother Kali Ma which she gave me during state of deep meditation in the winter of 1997 was really complicated and highly time consuming, but it still had an awe-inspiring effect on those who witnessed it.

The power lay in its complexity, but after years of trying to understand what created this power, I realized that it would be easier to remove the difficulty than add more elements to the ritual; so, I made it simpler. Now any one can conduct this rite with a minimum amount of preparation. Although I have simplified the ritual greatly, it has lost none of its original ferocity and awe-inspiring nature.

When you call to the dark goddess, Mother Kali, beware - for no mere mortal body can contain her powerful energy. She is known as Dus Mahavidya, the Parabrahm itself, and it is said that not even the universe has enough space for her might!

Attempting to allow her entry into your body could prove fatal; only lesser spirits, local guardians (Kuldevi/Kuldevta), or devoted followers of Kali should attempt such a ritual with utmost caution.

You must be fully committed to this ritual if you want to succeed, for it will require tremendous dedication, strength and unwavering faith that may span years of hard work before you can reap the rewards of your labour.

Do not risk yourself; if done incorrectly, the consequences will be dire and irreparable. Perform this ritual at your own risk!

Let's begin!

Stage 1:

Meditation Close your eyes and take a deep breath. Visualize the image of the Mighty Kali Ma in your mind's eye. Observe what thoughts and emotions arise within you. Meditate on her image and allow yourself to fully connect with her energy. Sit in a quiet place and focus your mind on Kali Ma. Visualize her image or a representation of her and repeat her mantra, "Om Krim Kalikayai Namah," Keep repeating the chant with all your might until it reverberates through the air, permeating every living being with its profound energy.

Stage 2:

Self-Reflection, reflect on your inner self and ask yourself some thought-provoking questions. Where are you suppressing your wild self? Is there an area in your life where you're playing it safe instead of expressing your true, angry, or enraged self? Allow yourself to be honest and truthful with yourself.

Stage 3:

Asana Take the goddess squat pose and let out several primal roars from your belly. Allow yourself to embody the fierce energy of the goddess and release any repressed emotions or frustrations.

Stage 4:

Offering to Kali Visualize yourself bowing down to Kali and offering her your limiting beliefs, negative thoughts, and emotions for her to destroy. Surrender to her and allow her to free you from any mental or emotional limitations that are holding you back.

Stage 5:

Journaling with Kali Take out your journal and connect with the energy of Kali. Ask her what she has to teach you. How does she express herself in your life? In what ways are you suppressing her energy? What do you think needs to be destroyed in your life to make way for new growth and transformation? Allow yourself to receive her wisdom and guidance.

Stage 6:

Embracing Vegetarianism, to fully embrace the teachings and energy of Kali, it is necessary to adopt a vegetarian diet. This means giving up all meat and dairy products, including fish and eggs. In addition, it is essential to refrain from alcohol and smoking in any form. Engaging in sexual activity is also not advised. Your soul must be pure and free from any toxins to fully connect with the energy of the Mighty Kali Ma. It is crucial to cultivate a clean and healthy lifestyle to honour the divine essence within you and around you. There can be no half-measures or shortcuts on this path. By making this commitment, you honour and respect all living beings and align yourself with the compassionate energy of the goddess.

Stage 7:

The Practice of Fasting To deepen your connection with the energy of Kali, fasting is recommended. However, it is crucial to consult with your doctor or medical practitioner before starting any fasting regimen, especially if you have any medical conditions. The fasting practice involves abstaining from food for 12 hours a day, with only water allowed. Start your fast from the moment you wake up and continue for a full 12 hours. It's important to avoid junk food and takeaways and to prepare your meals yourself. Drink plenty of mineral or filtered water during your fast to stay hydrated and nourished. Fasting can be a powerful tool for spiritual growth and inner purification, but it should be done with caution and care.

Stage 8:

Removing Falsehoods from Your Life To fully embrace the energy of Kali, it is necessary to remove all forms of falsehood from your life. This could mean limiting or eliminating activities such as watching TV, listening to music, playing video games, or engaging in other distractions that do not serve your highest good. It is up to you to decide what needs to be removed from your life to align with the energy of the goddess. Of course, you should keep what is necessary to make a living and support yourself. Take some time to reflect on what habits and activities are not serving your spiritual growth and consider making changes to live more authentically and in alignment with your true self.

Stage 9:

Embodying the Energy of Kali Once you have incorporated the practices outlined in previous chapters, it is time to focus on embodying the energy of Kali in your daily life. This involves cultivating a deep connection with the goddess and allowing her energy to flow through you. It means embracing your inner power, fearlessness, and intensity, while remaining compassionate and grounded. To embody the energy of Kali, it is essential to live in alignment with your highest self, speaking your truth, and taking action aligned with your values. Remember that embodying the energy of Kali is a lifelong journey, and it takes time, patience, and dedication. But the rewards are immeasurable, as you tap into your full potential and live your life with purpose and passion.

Stage 10:

Puja: Perform a puja, a traditional Hindu ritual, to honour Kali Ma. Offer flowers, incense, and food to her image or representation, and recite her mantras.

Stage 11:

Chanting: Chanting Kali Ma's mantras, such as "Om Kali Ma," "Om Hrim Shrim Klim Adya Kalika Param Eshwari Swaha," or "Om Kreem Kalikaye Namah," can help you connect with her energy and receive her blessings.

Stage 12:

Offerings: Offer items that are sacred to Kali Ma, such as black or red flowers, vermilion powder, or fruits like pomegranate, to her image or representation

Stage 13:

Practice Devotion: Devotion is a key element in building a deeper connection with Kali Ma. Regularly offer her puja, recite her mantras, and spend time meditating on her image or representation.

Stage 14:

Serve others: Kali Ma is also associated with compassion and service to others. Look for ways to serve others in your community and embody her compassionate nature in your actions.

Stage 15:

Prayer in English, translated from Sanskrit: Repeat this simple pray every day to bring you closer to Mother Kali.

"O Mother Kali, dark and fierce, Embodiment of time, death, and rebirth, I surrender myself to your transformative power. Guide me through the darkness and lead me to the light.

With your sword and your trident, cut away all that no longer serves me, and help me let go of attachments and fears. Teach me to embrace change and transformation.

Protect me from all harm and negativity, and help me cultivate inner strength and resilience. May your compassionate nature inspire me to serve others, and may your divine wisdom guide me on my spiritual path.

O Mother Kali, I offer myself to you completely, with all my strengths and weaknesses, all my hopes and fears, all that I am and all that I hope to be.

May your blessings fill my heart and soul, and may I always be in your divine presence, Now and forevermore. Om Kali Ma."

Stage 16:

Asking Mother Kali to enter your soul:

Do this when you are ready and feel you have mastered all the following tasks.

Using a red marker pen, write the following words below on to some clean white paper to the best of your ability. Don't worry about achieving perfection, just do what works best for you. Then, place the paper into a black pouch and secure it with red string. Finally, attach a black cord to the pouch around your neck. Wear this pouch all times, unless bathing.

"ॐ ह्रीं क्रीं श्रीं कालिकायै नमः॥ नमः कालिकायै नमः कालिकायै॥ सर्व मङ्गल माङ्गल्ये शिवे सर्वार्थ साधिके। शरण्ये त्र्यम्बके गौरि नारायणि नमोऽस्तु ते॥"

Sanskrit Translation:

"Om Hreem Kreem Shreem Kalikayai Namah|| Namah Kalikayai Namah Kalikayai|| Sarva Mangala Mangalye Shive Sarvartha Sadhike| Sharanye Tryambake Gauri Narayani Namostute||"

English Translation:

"Om, I bow to the Goddess Kali, the dark Mother. Salutations to Kali, salutations to Kali. Oh! The one who brings auspiciousness, who is auspicious herself, who is the consort of Shiva, who fulfils all desires, I take refuge in you, O three-eyed Gauri (Parvati), Narayani, I bow to you."

Stage 17:

Divine Soul Awaking Water - Kali Ma:

Master Rite to Call the Mighty Kail Ma to appear

In the depths of winter, in the year of 1998, Mother Kali Ma bestowed upon me a gift beyond measure - a mighty potion of incomparable power! Such an honour is not bestowed lightly, and my heart still swells with pride and gratitude at the mere thought of it. This elixir is more than a mere potion; it is a divine manifestation of the goddess's immense love and grace. Its power is beyond measure, and its potency is beyond compare. With a single sip, one can feel the very essence of the universe coursing through their veins, igniting a fire that burns brighter than a thousand suns! Such is the power of this elixir, a gift from the goddess herself, and I am forever humbled and awestruck by its majesty.

Behold, the magnificent "Divine Soul Awaking Water - Kali Ma"! Let these words stir your heart with passion and excitement, for this sacred elixir is no ordinary potion. It carries the power to awaken your very soul and set it ablaze with divine inspiration. Embrace its energy with fervour, and let it guide you on a journey of self-discovery and spiritual enlightenment. Kali Ma, the goddess of transformation, beckons you to take a sip and embark on a transformative path towards your truest, most authentic self.

Warning:

Do not begin making this divine potion until you have successfully completed all the preliminary tasks outlined in this book. Failure to do so will have dire consequences for your life, as you will not have undergone the essential soul-cleansing process required to commune with Kali Ma. There are no shortcuts on this journey, and attempting to take one will result in ruin.

1. Take a 500ml bottle of clear mineral water, pour the water in a clear bowl, now place the bowl in your temple or place of worship.

2. Add two drops of olive oil to the water

3. Next add one whole green chilli to the water, do not cut, just add it to the water whole.

4. Now place your hands over the water and say with passion:

(I have translated this from Sanskrit to English)

"Oh, mighty and benevolent Mother Kali Ma,

We humbly beseech thee to bless this holy water,

With thy divine touch and sacred grace.

May this water be infused with thy power and energy,

And become a potent elixir of transformation and healing.

May it cleanse our bodies, minds, and spirits of all impurities,

And awaken within us the spark of divinity that resides within.

Oh, Kali Ma, the goddess of change and transformation,

Guide us on the path of enlightenment and self-discovery,

And grant us the strength and courage to overcome all obstacles.

Bless this holy water, O Mother of the Universe,

And let it be a beacon of light and hope for all who seek thy divine blessings.

Jai Kali Ma!

1. Next, cover the water with some plate or clean cloth overnight.
2. Now, next morning, uncover the water bowl, drain out the water and remove the green chilli and carefully pour the water in to an empty bottle, try not to drop any of the water to the ground.
3. It is now ready!
4. Drink two drop of the Kali Ma water every day, once in the morning and one before retiring to bed.

5. Please note at the start this divine water may give you dizziness and headaches, is this occasion, do not drive or use machinery.

6. This elixir will awaken your soul and invite the powerful presence of Kali Ma to enter your soul. You may experience vivid dreams or find yourself imbued with the ability to run great distances effortlessly and without explanation.

7. Do not allow anyone else to use this divine water! Keep it locked away! Hidden from all eyes!

8. In the coming months, you will undergo a profound transformation that will leave you feeling as though your very soul no longer belongs to you. You will be imbued with extraordinary power, your mind will operate with lightning speed, and others will view you with a mixture of awe and fear, as though you have become something beyond human. Your physical body will undergo changes as well, rendering you stronger and more self-assured in your daily interactions and conversations.

9. This is the moment you have been waiting for your entire life. No longer will you be the timid individual who accepts the demands of others without question and allows them to treat you disrespectfully. You will stand tall and meet the gaze of everyone you encounter, empowered by a supernatural force not of this world. No longer will you be underestimated or mistreated, for you will radiate an aura of unshakable confidence and strength.

Stage 18:

Kali Ma - Mirror of Darkness:

This is now the final part to make Mother Kali Ma the bringer of death and destruction to appear in front of you. This may take several attempts before you are successful. Preform this rite at 3am any day, during a full moon.

1. Have a large full-size oval mirror looking similar shape to one below.

2. Write the words in a red maker pen कालीः जीवनम् in the centre.

3. Light two red candles and two black and place them behind you.

4. Light some nice smelling incense to fill the room.

5. Place some fresh red flowers in a vase.

6. Take a moment to unwind. Inhale through your nostrils and exhale through your mouth.

7. Next, raise your arms above your shoulders and say out loud with passion!

"OM KALI MATA, KRIPAYA MERE SAMNE PRAKAT HON!

8. Take a moment to relax, close your eyes for a minute or two.

9. As you open your eyes, you may notice that the room feels colder, or hear the distant beat of a drum. However, do not be alarmed if you don't perceive anything. You may also feel your body swaying or experience powerful sensations coursing throughout your being.

10. Say out loud:

(Translated from Sanskrit)

*"Oh, Mother Kali, the embodiment of power and destruction, I offer my humble prayers to you. Your fierce form strikes terror in the hearts of demons and evil-doers, and your compassionate form brings solace and salvation to the devotees. You are the divine mother who bestows strength, courage, and protection to your children. May your grace and blessings be upon me, and may I walk in your path of righteousness and truth. Jai Kali Ma!"
Appear to me now!*

11. You will now see smoke and a bright portal opening from the mirror, different coloured lights will start appearing from the ceiling and smell earth and a beautiful aroma not of this world filling the room. You may also hear the sound rattle of snakes. When this happens, kneed and give thanks to her majesty queen mother Kali Ma!

12. You can now ask mother Kali Ma any questions. Under no circumstances should you look directly into Kali Ma's eyes.

13. Once, you have finished asking Kali Ma questions, close the portal

14. Bow down, and give thanks to Kali Ma and step back and say once:

*Om kreem kreem kreem hum hum hreem
hreem dakshine kaalike kaalike swaha*

English translation: May the divine blessings of Kali Ma be upon us all. Go in peace!

The portal will now close and the lights in the room may flicker.

It is now finished!

Turn all the lights on.

CONCLUSION:

Dear reader, I am deeply grateful for your purchase of this lifetime work dedicated to the mighty Kali Ma! I salute you for embarking on this journey towards self-discovery and empowerment.

Throughout this book, I have strived to present the teachings of Kali Ma in their raw, unfiltered form. I have even gone to great lengths to translate ancient Sanskrit texts into English, although some passages proved too complex to translate. Nevertheless, I have endeavoured to maintain the authenticity of the original material.

Now, the Grimoire is complete, and you hold in your hands a powerhouse of forbidden knowledge lost in time. This is the first time that it has been made available to the general public, and I can assure you that you won't find anything like it anywhere else.

Please note that this book should not be shared with others or lent out for free, as there is a high probability that you may not receive it back. The pages alone contain power beyond the black flame, and just by possessing this mighty Grimoire of Kali Ma, you are attracting her presence into your life and everyday affairs.

This book is for everyone, regardless of age or religion. You do not need to be a practicing Hindu or a devotee of Kali Ma to benefit from its teachings. It transcends the concepts of good and evil or black and white magic.

Contrary to popular depictions in movies and books, Kali Ma is not a terrifying demon. She is a loving goddess who is firm but fair. She will help you grow and become your true self. If you are feeling timid and unconfident, unable to say no to simple requests from those who do not respect you or think of you only when they need something, Kali Ma will make you strong and teach you true power. You will no longer be disrespected or made to feel small. Instead, you will become a powerhouse of strength and knowledge, empowered to take on any challenge that comes your way.

I wish you all the best on your journey with Kali Ma, and I am honoured to have played a small part in it. May her loving presence guide you towards a fulfilling and empowered life.

Jai Kali Ma!

www.ingramcontent.com/pod-product-compliance
Lightning Source LLC
Chambersburg PA
CBHW041219070526
44584CB00001B/19